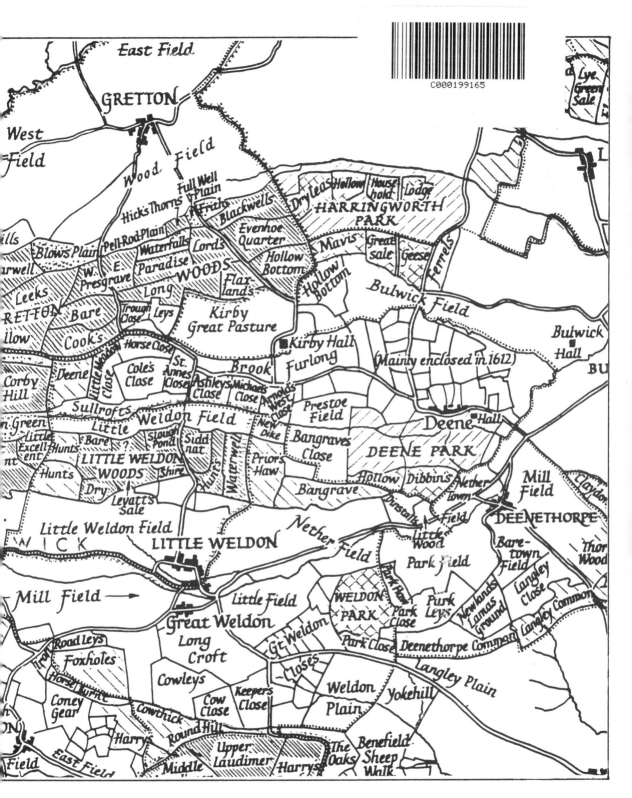

Detail from 17th-century map of Rockingham Forest. Reproduced by permission of the Record Society.

CORBY
A Pictorial History

Councillor Mrs. Margaret Mawdsley, the first mayor of Corby,
pictured on 1 March 1993, the day that Corby gained Borough status.

CORBY
A Pictorial History

Ron Sismey

John
I hope the book will bring back many memories.
Please enjoy it.
Ron
February 1994

Phillimore

1993

Published by
PHILLIMORE & CO. LTD.
Shopwyke Manor Barn, Chichester, Sussex

ISBN 0 85033 861 1

Printed and bound in Great Britain by
BIDDLES LTD.
Guildford, Surrey

Dedicated to Amy Elizabeth,
our first grandchild

List of Illustrations

Frontispiece: The first mayor of Corby Borough

Illustration Acknowledgements

British Steel/R. Sismey collection: 6a, 10a, 26-28, 30, 44-56, 60a, 68, 69a-c, 76, 77a-c, 78-82, 83 (courtesy of Mr. R. V. Thomas), 84-97, 104, 106-109, 113-116, 119-127, 129, 133, 134a & b, 137-141.

R. Sismey collection: 1 (courtesy of Mrs. P. Drage), 4b, 6b (courtesy of Mrs. M. Woolmer), 10b, 15, 19, 22 (courtesy of Mr. A. Phillips), 24 (courtesy of Mr. W. Carlyle), 29, 31 (courtesy of Mr. R. Williams), 32-34, 36, 37, 39, 41, 57, 58a & b, 59b-d, 60b (courtesy of Mrs. A. Tester), 60c, 63 (courtesy of Monseignor P. McAleenan), 64 (courtesy of Mr. G. Nichol), 70-73, 75, 117 (courtesy of Mr. J. Douglas), 118a & b, 130, 131, 136 (courtesy of Mr. J. Dilley).

Mr. R. J. Mears: 2, 8, 16a, 17, 42, 59a, 61, 103, 105, 144, 145, 147-150.

Mrs. R. Sumpter: 3, 16b, 23, 25a & b, 74, 98.

Mr. W. Boon: 4a, 5, 7, 9, 11-14, 18, 20, 21, 35, 38, 40, 62.

Arnold Photography: 43, 77d.

Corby Development Corporation: 65a & b, 66, 67, 99-102, 110-112.

Corby Evening Telegraph: frontispiece, 132 (courtesy of Mrs. A. Freeman), 135.

R.S. Components: 143.

Corby Borough Council: 128, 142, 146.

The Record Society: front endpaper.

Ordnance Survey: back endpaper.

Foreword and Acknowledgements

In writing this book it became obvious that the full history of Corby could not be told in just one volume and it is hoped that a second book may one day be produced to show the in-depth history of iron and steelmaking operations in the town.

In selecting photographs to cover the 100-year period of photography in the book, it was hoped not to use any that had been published before but several are of such importance that they are included. In attempting to put names and dates to some of the photographs it is realised that there may be other opinions and apologies are offered if there are any in error. I also apologise if any copyright ownership exists on any of the photographs of which I have not been aware.

I am thankful for advice and assistance given to me by Bob Mears, Greg Evans, Bill Boon, Rita Sumpter and Corby Borough Council. For help with the preparation of photographs, captions and written history my sincere thanks are passed to: Peter Hill, Alan Phillips, Bob Mears and Mavis Day plus all those listed who have loaned their photographs. The processing of all the script has been undertaken by a good friend, Ann Crighton, to whom due thanks are offered.

Finally, a tribute is paid to the many photographers who, at one time, were employed by Stewarts and Lloyds and the British Steel Corporation and whose work has made a large number of the photographs in the book possible. Their work could not have been published without the kind permission of British Steel's Tubes businesses, Corby.

Corby Milestones

1086		Corby recorded in Domesday Book as 'Corbie'.
1220		Right to hold a market and two fairs granted by King Henry III.
1585		Charter granted by Queen Elizabeth I.
1670		Charter re-confirmed by King Charles II after the Restoration of the Monarchy.
1862		First Pole Fair recorded.
1879		Opening of the Kettering to Manton railway line and Weldon and Corby station.
1881		Production of ironstone begins by the Cardigan Ironstone Company who were soon taken over by the Lloyds Ironstone Company.
1895		First steam excavator introduced to quarrying.
1903		Stewarts & Lloyds formed with head office in Glasgow.
1910	1 May	First iron made at the Corby blast furnaces of Lloyds Ironstone Company.
1917		Third blast furnace built.
1919	31 March	Alfred Hickman Ltd. acquires Lloyds Ironstone Company.
1920	30 October	Stewarts & Lloyds acquire Alfred Hickman Ltd. and the Corby site.
1932	29 November	S&L announce the iron, steel and tubemaking development at Corby is to go ahead.
1934	8 May	The rebuilt no.1 blast furnace is lit.
	15 June	First of the Glebe coke ovens goes into production.
	7 November	No.1 strip mill commences rolling. First continuous weld tubes made. No.2 blast furnace lit.
	27 December	First steel made in the Bessemer plant.
1935	8 May	No.3 blast furnace lit.
1936	September	Samuel Lloyd School opens.
1937	29 June	No.4 blast furnace lit.
1939	January	Lancashire & Corby Steel Manufacturing Company cold strip mill opened.
	March	Corby Urban District Council formed.
	30 July	First electric furnace steel made.
1949	8 December	First steel made by the open hearth process.
1950	May	Corby designated a New Town spearheaded by the Corby Development Corporation.
1951	July	First British giant walking dragline begins operating.
1961	18 September	New Deene coke ovens produce their first coke.
1965	3 July	First steel made by the basic oxygen steelmaking process (B.O.S.).

1966	22 January	Bessemer steelmaking ceases.
1967	28 July	Iron and steel industry nationalised; S&L becomes part of the British Steel Corporation (B.S.C.).
1971	18 September	Lancs. & Corby cold strip mill closes.
1974	May	Corby Urban District Council becomes the Corby District Council.
1978	1 April	C.D.C. takes over the housing functions of the Development Corporation.
1979	9 February	B.S.C. announces iron and steel production will cease at Corby.
	1 November	B.S.C. confirms closure.
	December	Nos.2 and 3 blast furnaces shut down in preparation for national strike.
	December	Assisted Area status granted to the town.
1980	3 January	Last ironstone loaded at the Corby quarries.
	7 January	Glebe coke ovens close.
	14 February	Deene coke ovens close.
	31 March	Corby Development Corporation hands over to the Commission for the New Towns who, over the next 12 years, were to build new industrial estates and over 200 factory units.
	21 April	Last iron tapped from no.4 blast furnace after national strike ends.
	22 April	Last steel produced from the B.O.S. plant.
	21 December	Last steel produced from the electric furnaces.
1981	22 June	England's first Enterprise Zone opened by the Secretary for the Environment, Michael Heseltine.
1983		Corby becomes a Parliamentary constituency.
1993	1 March	Corby is granted Borough status to become Corby Borough Council.

1. Early History and the Old Village

IF ANYONE LIVING in Corby in the 19th century could return to it today, it would be interesting to see their reaction to the way it has changed since then: they would hardly recognise most of the place! The changes that have occurred since the 1870s have been monumental, transforming a relatively quiet weaving and agricultural village of about seven hundred inhabitants into a vast industrial complex with a current population of about fifty-five thousand.

The story begins in the Bronze Age. The area around and including what is now Corby was certainly inhabited by tribes of that period, as pottery finds have testified. Settlement continued throughout the Iron Age/Romano-British period, during which the Colchester to Leicester road was built, part of which passed close to the present town centre.

The area at that time was densely forested. Rockingham Forest, much larger than it is today, virtually surrounded what was to become the Corby of the future. Today only remnants of this great forest remain right on the town's outskirts.

The Anglo-Saxons seem to have bypassed Corby, preferring to settle in nearby Cottingham, Snatchill and Desborough. The Vikings, however, in the ninth century, seem to have relished life here as they swept across the country establishing the 'Danelaw' and settlements like Rothwell and Apethorpe. The chief of one Danish group, Kori, gave his name to a settlement made in a clearing in Rockingham Forest: 'Koris by'—Kori's village ('-by' is a commonplace name ending in Scandinavia, particularly in Denmark). The Viking group would have found an ideal place for their way of life; timber for their boats and houses, springs and brooks for water, game in the forest, fertile land and the rivers Welland and Nene were all close by.

Though many Vikings returned to Scandinavia in later years, a significant number inter-married with the native 'locals' and became Englishmen, accepting the Saxon, Edward the Elder, as king. Kori's name, like that of many other chieftains, remained associated with the settlement, and with spelling and pronunciation changes was corrupted to today's Corby.

Many Saxon earls owned huge tracts of land in the country. One of them, Siward, a right-hand man of Edward the Confessor, had much of the Corby area under his control and, after the Norman invasion of 1066, his son married the new landowner, Countess Judith, niece of William I. He was, however, to come to a sticky end in 1076, when Judith falsely betrayed him as a conspirator against the king.

William I had a castle built on a hill above Rockingham, just outside Corby, to symbolise his power and authority, and to use as an administration centre to protect his new lands. Named Rockingham Castle, it commanded a wide expanse of land below and gave sweeping views for miles around, providing ample warning should potential insurgence occur. Corby was now recognised as a Royal Manor and the forest was to become a favourite hunting ground of many Norman and Plantagenet kings.

On the religious front, Corby's first church—still existing in the original village—was built mainly in the early 13th century. Its original name of St Peter's was changed to John the Baptist in 1900. At nearby Pipewell one of the largest Cistercian abbeys in Britain was built in 1142 and 13 monks were installed. In 1189 King Richard I held his first Great Council there, attended by most of the English nobility and higher clergy, to raise money for the Crusades.

An event occurred around 1220 which was of great consequence for Corby as it started a tradition which continues to this day. Henry, son of Robert Braiboc (who had been given the Royal Manor at Corby in 1205 by King John) was granted the right to hold two annual fairs and a weekly market. One of these fairs, Whitsuntide Fair, still exists, although over the years it has lost its annual function and is now held every 20 years in the old village. Known as the Pole Fair, it includes an ancient custom whose origins appear to have Viking roots. Before every fair, barricades were erected across the entries to the village; anyone wishing to gain access was stopped by a 'gatekeeper' who demanded payment by a toll. Those who refused were carried off to the stocks—women by chair and men by means of a pole.

The Pole Fair took place, like many markets and other public meetings, in the Jamb (the name is probably a variation of 'jambe', the French for 'leg', the language spoken by the Normans) which is at the junction of High Street and Rockingham Road. The old village sprang up around this area and, until the 1870s, was where all the businesses were based.

There are records of a number of poachers and outlaws in the Corby area—the surrounding thick woodland offered them ample cover—and also the punishments inflicted on those caught, ranging from loss of life or limb to heavy fines or imprisonment for a year and a day. However, according to legend, Queen Elizabeth I got lost in the woodland and was safely led to the village by outlaws! Be that as it may, the Queen granted Corby a Charter in 1585 for 'services rendered', which gave the men of Corby privileges such as 'the exemption from tolls and certain (feudal) duties'. What is more probable is that the Charter was granted as a gift to her favourite magistrate, former captain of the bodyguard and later Lord Chancellor, Sir Christopher Hatton, then Lord of Corby Manor, who resided at nearby Kirby Hall. This is still an outstanding building, although partially ruined, and can be visited all year round. It is in the care of English Heritage.

The 17th century was a time of national turmoil and the Civil War left its impression locally. Rockingham was Royalist but nearby Great Oakley was Parliamentarian; two cousins on opposite sides, one in the castle and the other at Oakley Hall, settled matters 'amicably' and with due courtesy towards each other! On a wider regional basis, however, some men from the Corby area were wounded or killed in battle and there are some records of compensation paid to needy families.

After the Civil War and period of the Commonwealth under Cromwell, King Charles II confirmed Queen Elizabeth's Charter in 1670. The Hattons exchanged land with the Brudenell family of Deene Hall, including the lordship of the Corby Manor which still remains with that family today. This family boasted one famous member, the 7th Earl of Cardigan who, in 1854, led the Charge of the Light Brigade in the Crimean War.

In the latter part of the 17th century the first main manufacturing industry sprang up in Corby; handloom weaving, which was to blossom in the next century, established the village as a weaving centre. The oldest houses existing in the vicinity of High Street and Meeting House Lane date from these times.

The weaving industry went from strength to strength during the 18th century when, with farming, it became the chief occupation of the village. The 19th century was a different matter. During the first half of the 1800s the handloom weaving industry collapsed because of competition and increased output from big industrial mills. The village did not recover for a long time and many unemployed villagers had to seek work elsewhere—a difficult task locally. As a result poverty and hard times hit Corby and its population of over seven hundred. Agricultural depression and the enclosure of Corby's common fields in 1829-31 added to the misery.

Slowly Corby recovered. Then the 1870s brought a series of events which transformed the village forever—the coming of the railway, the development of ironstone extraction and brickmaking. In 1875-79 the building of the Kettering to Manton (Rutland) railway, though less than 16 miles long, connected Corby with the main industrial towns of the Midlands, provided employment for 1,500 and brought new trades to the village. Timber and bricks were required in copious quantities, so Rockingham Forest was plundered and local clay pits were dug. Tradesmen arrived to feed the hungry workers; brewers' drays, fishmongers, pedlars, bakers and butchers became common sights. A 'shanty town' sprang up with somewhat overcrowded 'huts' to accommodate workers and their families.

Despite the squalid conditions, regular and relatively good pay was taken home—up to £2 10s. each week for a bricklayer. By the time the railway opened in 1879 the Corby Tunnel alone had needed 20 million bricks in its construction. When the railway had been built and most of the itinerant workers had left, the village settled down with a population of 785 in 1881, four pubs and numerous thatched cottages.

Brickmaking and ironstone quarrying became the main source of employment for the remainder of the century. The people of this time were thus the original pioneers of heavy industry which they had brought to a village which had only ever previously known rural crafts and industries.

1.   Photograph of the Roman pottery kiln taken by Dr. Arthur Stokes in 1903, when the kiln was discovered during ironstone excavations to the right of the Corby to Weldon road. It was originally thought that the discovery might be a cremation from the Bronze Age, as one had been found in 1890 in ironstone excavations only a few hundred yards away. Dr. Stokes was a surgeon who lived at Cheyne House, Weldon and his practice covered many of the local villages from 1880-1924. He was also the medical officer for the Lloyds Ironstone Company.

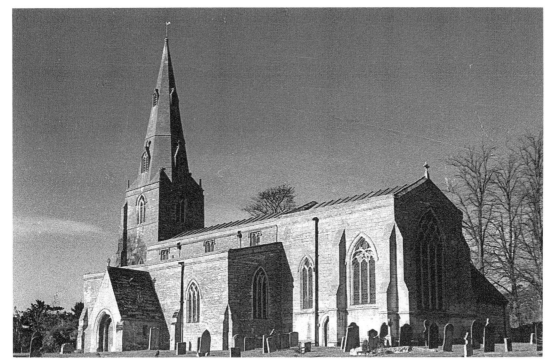

2.　The tower of the church of St John the Baptist is the oldest part of the building, dating back to the 13th century, with the spire and other parts either 14th or 15th century. The church was much restored after the arrival of the Rev. T. G. Clarke in 1897 who, it is written, 'provided seating'. Until the end of December 1899 the church was dedicated to St Peter as with the other village churches of the Cardigan Estate at Deene and Stanion. It is recorded that from January 1900 it was changed to St John the Baptist so that the rector could also attend feast services at St Peter's, Deene for which he was also responsible at that time.

3.　Members of the Corby Brass Band seen *c.*1902. *From left, back row:* Fred Marshall, Rowlatt, Joseph Streather; *middle row:* Fred Brooks, Dixon, Ted Bailey, Walter Rowlatt, George Rowlatt, Willie Davies, Jim Rowlatt; *front row:* Bill Cottingham, Joe Robinson, Mr. Rice (bandmaster), Clow, Ted Simmons, Jack Dixon.

4a. The High Street in 1914 looking west showing, on the left, the original *Nag's Head* and the Co-op shop. Both these buildings were to be cement-rendered before being demolished and replaced. Many of the buildings on the right still stand today.

'NAG'S HEAD' INN,
CORBY.

PROPRIETOR - A. TILLEY.

Phipps' Noted Ales and Stout.

GOOD ACCOMMODATION FOR CYCLISTS & PRIVATE PARTIES.

BEST CIGARS.

WINES & SPIRITS OF THE FINEST QUALITY.

Ten Commandments of A. TILLEY'S Establishment.

1.—Thou shalt come to mine house when thou art thirsty.

2.—Thou shalt always keep my name in thy memory.

3.—Thou shalt visit me often on week days.

4.—Thou shalt honour me when I deserve it, so that thou mayest live long, and continue drinking in my house.

5.—Thou shalt neither break nor destroy anything in my house ; if thou dost, thou shalt pay me each time double for it.

6.—Thou shalt not make any disturbance in my house, for such things are distasteful to me.

7.—Thou shalt not steal anything from me. I need all I have myself.

8.—Thou shalt not dare to pass counterfeit coin or money on me.

9.—Thou shalt not expect large or full glasses, because the landlord has to live off the profit.

10.—Thou shalt, after thou hast been eating or drinking at my house, pay me honestly for it, for the landlord never likes to have anything to do in the chalk line.

4b. The business card of A. Tilley, landlord of the *Nag's Head* in 1905.

5. Looking down the High Street to the east, *c.*1910. The parked wheeled vehicle was the village bier, used to carry coffins to the funeral service, first to the parish church and then the long walk up the Rockingham Road Hill to the cemetery.

6a.   Taken in 1911 in the Jamb, with some of the schoolchildren of the time; part of the *Cardigan Arms* pub is seen on the left. There were also pubs named *Cardigan Arms* in Stanion and Deenethorpe, being so named after the Cardigan family of Deene Park who were Lords of the Manor of all three villages.

6b.   A group of children in 1907 with their teachers at the Rowlett School.

7. Stanion Lane seen in *c*.1915 was the main road into the village from the Kettering direction. The cottages were demolished in 1934 when the road was widened but the brick houses built *c*.1908 still remain.

8. A late Victorian view of the Weldon Road cottages with the steeple of the parish church in the background. Note the washing drying on the bushes and the road surface of crushed stone. In the years before the cottages were demolished to make way for the roundabout in 1970, Jim Brothwell ran his boot repair shop in the cottage on the left.

9.　The village youth football team, known as the Swifts, seen here *c*.1910, are named as follows—*back row:* Johnny Blades, Frank Bates, William Hobnan, Walter Rowlatt, Bob Payne, Edwin Stimson; *middle row, kneeling*: William Rowlatt, Jim Peerless, Tom Wilford, Tom Fellows; *front row:* Harold Walker, Jim Loveday, Perce Brown.

10a. Taken in 1919, this is a view of the Jamb which was regarded as the centre for village activities. Apart from the brick houses on the left, all the others have disappeared. The house in the centre with the small shop belonged to the Payne family and was burnt down in the 1930s.

10b. Further into the Jamb and looking up the Rockingham Road towards the railway bridge. The Willowbrook duck pond is seen in the centre of the picture. The cottage at the entrance to Tunwell Lane, so named after the town well, shows a datestone of 1707 and, from the sign, was the home in 1919 of H. Peerless, bootmaker and repairer.

11.   The railway station, on the Kettering to Manton line, was opened in 1879. Initially it was known as the Weldon and Corby station to avoid confusion with the existing station in Corby, Lincolnshire. The line was closed to passenger traffic in 1966 but was briefly re-opened from April 1987 to June 1990 for an experimental shuttle service to Kettering.

12.   The dedication service of the war memorial took place in 1920, and was conducted by the Rev. T. G. Clarke. The background shows the Rowlett School which was rebuilt and re-opened on 27 April 1914. The war memorial was re-sited by the parish church in the early 1960s.

13.   The Corby Charter Band is pictured in 1922 in front of Corby House which was built in 1906 by James Pain, a benefactor in that his companies, James Pain Ironstone Company and the Weldon and Corby Brick Company, gave new life to the village from 1880. It was this house that Allan Macdiarmid, chairman of Stewarts & Lloyds, provided for the very successful Uppingham and Corby Boys Club in the 1930s. Mr. Macdiarmid's interest in the most unlikely linking of the Uppingham public school and an expanding steel town stemmed from the fact that he was educated at Uppingham School.

Top row: J. W. Rowlatt, J. Walker, S. Mason, L. Nicholls, J. Nicholls; *middle row:* A. Fellowes, C. W. Dixon, C. Dixon, W. White, A. Dixon, G. Wardell, L. Robinson, J. Brothwell, R. Dixon (treasurer); *front row:* F. Brooks, H. Stimson, W. Rowlatt, D. W. Pain (president), W. Boon (bandmaster), E. Bailey, W. Perrell, H. Boon.

14.   The ancient ceremony of letting the Town Land to the highest bidder took place annually. In this picture the ceremony is taking place in the Rowlett School, *c*.1918, in the presence of the parish council. At the beginning of the ceremony a pin was pushed through a candle stem which was then lit, and bids were taken for the rent of the land. The last bid received before the pin fell out of the candle was granted the land. The pin is about to fall out, which explains the anxiety of the farmers on the right. Members of the parish council from the left are: Bert Prentice, Joseph Streather, Albert Brooks (headmaster), John Sarrington (chairman), and William Boon. Others stand to get a better view.

15.   The first out-of-town branch of the Kettering Industrial Co-operative Society (K.I.C.S.), shown here in 1920, was opened in 1898 in a converted house in the High Street. It was replaced by larger premises in 1925. Mr. Walter Walker, the manager, is shown in the doorway with his staff.

16a. Lloyds cinema, which stood at the corner of Lloyds Road and Rockingham Road where there is a car-wash today, was a group of wooden buildings provided by the company. It acted as a social centre for the village until 1936. Apart from film shows many other activities took place; being advertised for 14 May 1933 is a supper and social for the price of two shillings.

16b. The full cast of a show is seen on-stage in the cinema; the musical accompaniment is by the Golden Melody Makers.

17.   Empire Day celebrations on 24 May 1929 at the Rowlett School featured, *from left, back row:* Lilly Battams, Gertie Lattimore, Lilly Underwood, Don Williams, Francis Dixon, Eileen Rowlett, Mrs. Gordon Pain; *front row:* Bob Mears, Jack Spriggs, Jack Rust.

18.   The girls choir at the Rowlett School are shown in 1931 with the assistant headmistress, Miss Florence Chapman, and headmaster, Albert Brooks. *From left, back row:* Hilda Ironmonger, Edna Walker, Violet Bailey, Muriel Walker, May Kerfoot, Doris Plowman, Nita Glithero, Peggy Germany, Audrey Sanders, Edith Fellows; *middle row:* Maisie Morris, Mabel Walker, Ada Longhurst, Hilda Walker, Florrie Plowman, Eileen Rowlatt, Irene Wood, Iris Ironmonger, Ivy Bowden, Betty Goodman; *front row:* Esme Drury, Vera Clarke, Irene Hornsey, Joyce Bailey, Cathy Lane, Hilda Beadsworth, Ruby Miller, Joan White.

19.   The efforts in the early 1930s of a team of 16 men on the horse-drawn and inefficient Corby fire engine to pump water from the duck pond of the Willowbrook in the Jamb appear to be enjoyable. The eventual arrival of George Dennet and crew with the modern Kettering engine still did not stop two thatched houses at the bottom of the Jamb burning down. The houses were rebuilt in brick and included the former shop of the Payne family who had occupied one of the houses.

20.   The *White Hart,* seen in the early 1930s when the village benefited from the new electricity supply. Before the decade had ended, the thatched pub and some adjoining cottages had been demolished to make way for a new *White Hart.*

21.   One of the characters of the village was Bill Bishop who ran his small barber's shop at the entry to the Jamb; the shop had a spiral staircase to reach the first floor. Mr. Bishop, seen here standing outside his shop *c*.1930, later had a large temporary building at the bottom of the Jamb where up to six hairdressers were always hard-worked.

22.   The Lloyds Ironstone Company built 16 cottages in Lloyds Road at the turn of the century for their quarry workers. The blast furnaces built in 1910 were to be some 200 yards away but the expansion of the 1930s and later almost surrounded the cottages. By this time they had been painted black and were close to the Glebe coke ovens. They were demolished from 1954.

23.   In 1934 the K.I.C.S. bought the property adjoining its own 1925 premises in the High Street for a butchery shop and a milk delivery service. Charles Rowlatt previously ran his butcher's shop from the house on the left with a dentist next door. The dentist's surgery was to move into a first-floor flat above Friend's flower and fruit shop which was next to Ricci's fish shop in the newly constructed block next door. Later the fish shop was owned for many years by the Browell family.

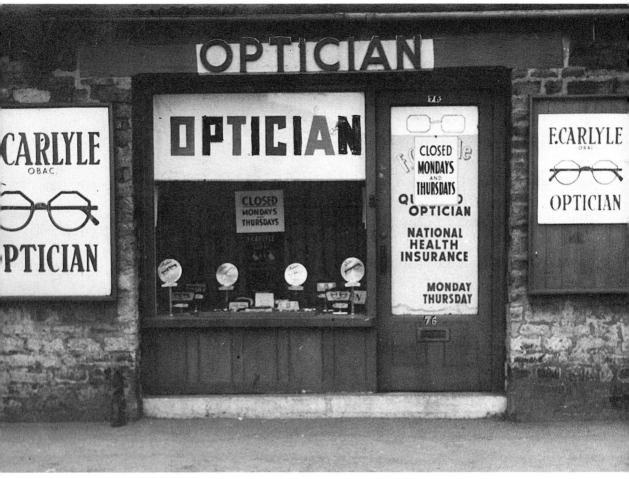

24.   Many of the existing businessmen prior to the 1930s expansion, such as the Sarrington and Boon families, continued to trade for many years. Other businesses were attracted by the upsurge in population. Typical was Corby's first resident optician, Frank Carlyle, who travelled two days a week from Leicester from 1933 to 1938, until he opened his first shop in a converted blacksmith's shop opposite the Rowlett School.

25a.   Corby cricket team, 1931. *Left to right, back row:* E. Streather, J. Graham, W. Dixon, C. Dixon, T. Fellows, J. Woolmer; *front row:* B. White, D. Perrell, A. Dixon, A. Fellows, W. Perrell.

25b.   Corby Football Club team of 1931/2. *Left to right, back row:* B. Bates, B. Dix (manager), E. Streather, J. Graham, T. King, D. Perrell, W. Whitehead, W. Marshall, C. Walker, H. Pullen (trainer); *front row:* W. Palliaser, A. Rowlett, A. Dixon, A. Mears, B. Marshall.

2. Lloyds Ironstone Company

BUILDING THE RAILWAY had kindled an interest in ironstone quarrying. The ironstone lay in great deposits around Corby and was to prove one of Britain's major sources. Knowledge of these deposits soon became widespread. One man in particular, Samuel Lloyd of Lloyd & Lloyd Ltd. in Birmingham, commissioned an agent to look at the ironstone and to report on its quality and possible use. A satisfactory report, despite high phosphorus content which made it unsuitable for contemporary steelmaking methods, led to Lloyds Ironstone quarrying the ore at Corby. The iron content of the ironstone averaged 28 per cent, a very lean figure.

Other individuals also had ironstone interests. Among them was James Pain who, later, owned the brick kilns at the 'Clayholes'. He uncovered the shallow ironstone beds by hand and took the product by horse and cart to the Weldon & Corby railway station for delivery to the foundries in various parts of the country.

Quarrying for ironstone had begun in many parts of the county after the 1851 Great Exhibition had shown that great deposits existed, even though its constituents demanded changes in smelting techniques. Blast furnaces in the county producing pig-iron for the foundries, particularly in the West Midlands and South Wales, were to follow the opening in 1853 of a blast furnace at Wellingborough. Of the eight blast furnaces already operating in 1880, four were at the local sites of Wellingborough, Islip, Cransley and Kettering and all these were to come under the control of Stewarts & Lloyds in Corby at a later stage. This company was formed in 1903 by the amalgamation of the Scottish tubemakers, A. & J. Stewart and Menzies Ltd., with the Birmingham tubemakers, Lloyd & Lloyd Ltd. It was not until 1920 that S&L, as they were known, were to gain control of the Lloyds Ironstone Company at Corby.

The Lloyds wished to develop their activities in the Corby area and a decision was taken to build two blast furnaces which made the first iron for foundries in May 1910. At that time it is recorded that the company had contracts to supply one million tons of ironstone for other smelters. The year 1911 saw a prolonged strike at the blast furnaces, connected with union recognition, which caused much strife in the village, for those both for and against the strike, with the police being accused of supporting the strike-breakers brought into the village.

As a result of high demand for iron production in the First World War an additional blast furnace was erected at Corby with government help. This came into production in 1917.

26. The ironstone bed at the bottom of the quarry was uncovered in the early days using the 'plank and barrow' method of manual working. The ironstone was loaded by hand into small trucks and then transferred into wagons for transportation from the railway station. The quarry is thought to have been behind the South Road; it belonged to James Pain. Dr. Stokes' daughter recalled in her writings that the doctor was called out on many emergencies to attend men who had fallen off the plank.

27. The first ever steam machine to be introduced to onstone quarries worked from 1895. Here the Wilson steam navvy can be seen removing the ironstone bed to load into wagons. These types of machines were much used in the construction of the Manchester ship canal.

28. Machines were also designed to remove the overburden where it became deeper. The Wilson no.2 steam face shovel was supplied in 1899 and is pictured in the 1950s after it had been rebuilt, operating in Prestons Pit alongside the Weldon Road. Today this area is the Weldon (South) Industrial Estate.

29.   The two blast furnaces pictured from the Rockingham Road bridge, *c*.1914. On the right, to the rear of the picture, can be seen the slag crushing plant which the Tarmac company took over in 1922.

30.   The three blast furnaces with the pig beds in front where the molten iron was poured through sand channels. When the iron had cooled and solidified it was manually loaded into wagons for despatch, using the barrows shown. The skip hoists to feed materials to each furnace can be seen to the rear of the furnaces.

31. Bert Payne in charge of the skip house where he controlled the supply of ironstone, coke and limestone into the bell at the top of the furnace. A working diagram of the double opening bell to feed the furnace is seen on the wall.

32.   This team of men worked for the Tarmac Roadstone Company and are pictured here *c.*1926 at the rear of the blast furnaces which produced the slag which, when cooled and tipped, formed the moulds shown. The men were known as 'the crackers' as their function was to break up the slag moulds with heavy hammers and load it into trucks for transport to the plant where it was crushed, sized and tar coated. The engine built by Andrew

Barclay & Sons, Kilmarnock in 1911 was driven by J. Brooks. Production was re-sited at a modern plant in Stanion Lane in 1938 where it continued to use the blast furnace slag until the source ran out in 1981. A few people can be identified: front row centre with cigarette, Bert Freeman, fifth from right in first standing row, Albert Wright, and extreme right in that row with collar and tie, Walter Carter.

3. Pole Fairs

THE ACCEPTED TRANSLATION of the Charter granted to Corby by Queen Elizabeth I in 1585 and read at various points at each Pole Fair:

ELIZABETH, By Grace of God, of England, Scotland, France and Ireland, Queen, Defender of the Faith etc. to all and singular Sheriffs, Mayors, Bailiffs, Constables, Ministers and all other her faithful subjects as well within the liberties as without, to whom these present letters shall come, greeting.

WHEREAS according to the custom hitherto obtained and used in our Kingdom of England the men and tenants of ancient demesne of the Crown of England are and ought to be quit of Toll, Pannage, Murage and Passage, throughout our whole Kingdom of England and according to the aforesaid custom the men and tenants of ancient demesne of the Crown aforesaid have always hitherto from the time whereof memory runneth not to the contrary been accustomed to be quit from contribution to the expenses of Knights coming to our Parliament or that of our Progenitors formerly Kings of England. For the community of the Commonality of the same Kingdom, also according to the same custom, the men and tenants of the manors, which are of ancient demesne of the Crown aforesaid ought not to be placed in any assizes, juries, or recognisances for the lands and tenements which they hold of the same demesne unless only in those which ought to be held in the courts of the same manors and for them.

WHEREAS the Manor of Corbei in the County of Northampton is of ancient demesne of our Crown of England, as is found by a certain certificate returned into our Chancery by the Treasurer and Chamberlain of our Exchequer, by our command thereupon.

WE ENJOIN and command you and every one of you that you permit all and singular the men and tenants of the Manor of Corbei aforesaid to be quit from such Toll, Pannage, Murage and Passage to be paid on account of their goods or things throughout our whole realm aforesaid and on account of the expenses of the Knights aforesaid. Also that you do not place the same men or tenants of the same manor in any assizes, juries or recognisances to be held out of the Court of such Manor against the aforesaid custom unless the lands and tenements be held of other tenure for which they ought to be placed in assizes, juries or recognisances according to the form of the statute of the Common Council of our Kingdom of England therefore provided. And if on these occasions or any of them you should make any distress on the aforesaid men and tenants of the Manor of Corbei aforesaid you shall without delay release the same to them.

IN WITNESS whereof we have caused these our letters to made patent. Witnessed ourselves at Westminster the Second day of December in the Twenty Seventh year of our Reign.

CORBY, KETTERING,

NORTHANTS.

THE

GREAT POLE FAIR

Held once in TWENTY YEARS,

To commemorate the Charter granted by H.M. Queen Elizabeth in 1585, and confirmed by H.M. King Charles II. in 1682, to the men and tenants of the Ancient Demesne of Corbei, in the County of Northampton, will be proclaimed on

WHIT-MONDAY, MAY 19th, 1902.

The POLE FAIR will be carried out in imitation of a

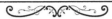

Village Fair in ye Olden Time.

Residents and Visitors will be carried in Mock State to the Stocks, and there confined till the Men of Corbei, exercising their just and Lawful Privilege, will without Order from the JUSTICE OF THE PEACE restore them to liberty.

☞ Toll will be demanded from all persons visiting the Fair or passing through the Village on that day.

An EFFICIENT BAND will be in attendance.

Commodious standing room for Travelling Theatres, Shows, Switchbacks, &c., can be obtained.

GOD SAVE THE KING.

The MIDLAND RAILWAY Co., will issue Cheap Tickets to Weldon and Corby Station from Leicester, Northampton, Bedford, Peterborough, Melton Mowbray, and intermediate Stations.

Chas. T. Hart, Printer and Bookbinder, Lindsay Street, Kettering.

33.   Many questions remain about the origins of the Pole Fair, which is first recorded in 1862, and why it is held every 20 years.

34.   Reading the proclamation at the 1902 fair on Whit Monday is the rector of Corby, the Rev. T. G. Clarke, seen on the left. The picture is taken from the churchyard at the junction of roads from Weldon and Stanion, leading into Church Street and South Road. The signpost also holds one of the paraffin oil street lamps.

35.   One of the three gates erected at the entrances to the village for the 1902 fair. Visitors had to pay a toll to gain access to the village or pay the price of being put in the stocks. The photograph was taken at the top of the High Street at the Cottingham Road and Station Road junction and includes a cycling club, a popular pastime in those days. 1902 was a year for celebrations: on 8 June, national celebrations were held for the end of the Boer War and on 9 August the Coronation of King Edward VII led to more rejoicing.

36.   Posing at the entrance to Stocks Lane at the 1902 fair stands a group of villagers. The ladies seem to be much more comfortable than the menfolk who were carried on a pole or 'stang'. The new Co-op shop is seen at the rear. The building behind the stocks is still a shop.

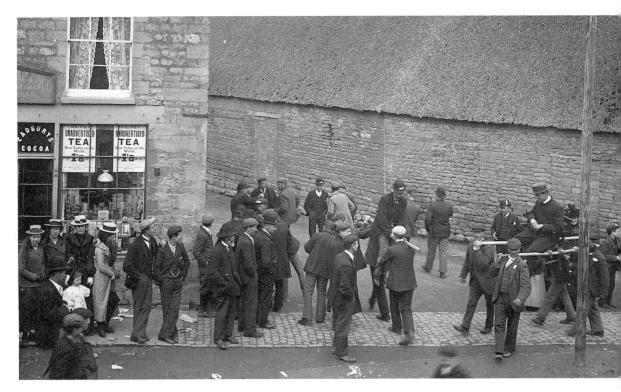

37.   The entrance to Stocks Lane at the 1922 fair. Note the twist on words of the two posters exhorting the public to drink 'unadvertised tea'.

38.   It is traditional for an Elizabethan pageant to be presented at each fair. In 1922 children from the Rowlett School performed. On the left is Colin Elliott as Sir Christopher Hatton; Colin later returned to be headmaster of the school. Queen Bess was played by Ruby Kendall with Lord Burleigh on her left played by Warren Smith and Sir Francis Drake on the right played by Arthur Bowden.

39.   In 1922 the stocks were erected outside the Rowlett School. Note the contribution box for paying the toll to be allowed out of the stocks. At the rear of the shop in the background was Mr. Patrick's bakery. The shop later became well known as the tuck shop for the children from Rowlett School.

40. Because of the Second World War there was no fair in 1942. However, the Charter was read by the Rev. Brooke Westcott. Being carried in a chair at the top of the Jamb is the chairman of the Urban District Council, Mr. Wilf Roe.

41. In 1947 a mock Pole Fair was held. Members of the parish church choir are, from left to right: Joan Ironmonger, Pauline Dixon, Rose Davis, Beryl Payne, May Meadows, Doreen Greetham, Mary Miller, Margaret Palliaser, Peggy Langley, Josie Bell, Margaret Wallace, Rene Davis and Joan Stafford. In the centre background the trombone player is Jim Roe.

42.   1962 saw massive crowds for the fair. In the stocks are: Dennis Cowley (chairman of the Urban District Council), Pat Stewart (the Pole Fair Queen), the Rev. Brooke Westcott and Colin Elliott (headmaster of Rowlett School). Standing behind the last two is Herbert Broad, the chairman of the Pole Fair Committee.

43.   Featured at the 1982 fair in the stocks at the *Cardigan Arms* are: the Rev. Ron Howe, Yvonne Russell (Pole Fair Queen) and Cllr. Jim Thomson (chairman of the District Council). Also shown, from left: Kitty Cooper (fair treasurer), Cllr. Kelvin Glendenning, George 'Buller' Dixon (oldest resident), Cllr. Joe Sims and Cllr. Mrs. Esther Donald. Some of the visitors from the twin town of Velbert, Germany are also included.

4. Works Development

IN 1910 S&L, the largest producer of steel pipes and tubes in the country, began to look at ways of producing ironstone and iron and steelmaking. The main focus of their attention was north Lincolnshire. The company was advised that open hearth steel would be more readily weldable, more so than Bessemer steel. By 1920 interest in building a steelworks in north Lincolnshire was diminishing due to many unforeseen circumstances. At the end of 1920, by acquiring Alfred Hickman Ltd., S&L had also gained control of the Lloyds Ironstone Company at Corby.

At this time S&L were also to become involved with Tarmac Ltd. to convert large quantities of blast furnace slag into tarmacadam for road-making. The company had a small plant working alongside the blast furnaces at Corby.

There were many trading difficulties by the mid-1920s as a consequence of the First World War, but S&L continued to search for means of producing more iron and steel from their vast acquired interests in ironstone. In 1927 it was first mooted that Corby should be the site for a fully integrated iron, steel and tubemaking complex, employing a modified Bessemer process to accommodate the high phosphorus content of the local ore.

Various reports were made by H. A. Brassert & Co. Ltd., an American based company, on S&L's many interests, which also extended to coal mines. By 1930 the company advised that, after a number of national sites were considered, Corby was the obvious choice for both Bessemer and open hearth steelmaking, using iron from new blast furnaces and leading to rolling mills and continuous weld tubemaking. Lengthy discussions took place within the S&L board, and such places as the Thames Estuary were favoured for the new site by some members, but the overriding consideration was the question of finance for such a project in which the Bank of England was involved.

By late 1930 a revised report by Brassert & Co. detailed a plan for the full integrated site, costing £5.7 million, and in April 1931 the full board considered the proposition further but decisions were delayed by the bankers. In late 1932 a letter was circulated to all shareholders setting out the decision that had been reached for the development of the Corby site and, almost immediately, appointments of the directors and superintendents for the projects were announced.

January 1933 saw the beginning of site clearance for the works area, much of which had already been quarried for ironstone, and an immediate reconstruction of no.1 blast furnace was begun by Ernest N. Wright, a subsidiary company from the West Midlands. Work also started on the Glebe coke ovens, ore preparation and sintering plants.

The initial success of the Corby scheme quickly led to further expansion from the mid-1930s with additional quarry diggers, no.4 blast furnace, coke ovens, rolling capacity and the opening of a cold strip rolling mill. At this time large quantities of excess coke oven gas were sold to the Kettering Gas Company which led to the closure of their gas works; other excesses had to be burnt off to atmosphere by the Corby 'candle'.

The whole basis of the plant at Corby was to produce steel tubes and the person given the task of seeing the plant constructed was Mr. Graham Satow who had moved from the Phoenix Works in Scotland. After much investigation it was decided to produce by the Fretz-Moon or Continuous Weld (C.W.) and the push bench seamless pipe methods. As regards production tonnages, the welded pipe initially from three mills far outstripped that of the seamless pipe.

The ever-threatening fear of a Second World War was to act as a spur to many of the decisions taken during the 1930s, and by the time it did arise in 1939 the whole complex was geared to ever increasing production tonnages. By that time production figures amounted to nearly two million tons of ironstone, 600,000 tons of iron, half a million tons of Bessemer steel and over 200,000 tons of finished tubes for the year.

44. This August 1933 photograph shows the progress and development of the new steelworks site; a vast amount of infilling was required on the future tubeworks site to the right of the picture. The coke-oven gas holder and Bessemer plant are above the tubeworks area. The first part of the main offices has already been completed in the centre of the picture. The stores and engineering shop progress are on the left.

45. Rebuilding of the no.1 blast furnace has started and other construction has begun on other plants, as seen from the Rockingham Road bridge.

46a.   On 8 May 1934 Miss Elspeth Macdiarmid, the youngest daughter of the chairman of Stewarts & Lloyds (S&L), lights the first of the blast furnaces, the former Lloyds Ironstone Company no.1 furnace.

46b.   Allan Macdiarmid became chairman of S&L on 1 July
1926, taking over from R. M. Wilson who had briefly
superseded John Graham Stewart. For some years prior to this
event and until the 1930s, lengthy negotiations had taken place
regarding the building of a large iron, steel and tubemaking
plant at a number of locations. With the enthusiasm of the
chairman, the final approval of the Board was given on
28 October 1932 for the project to begin on the Corby site.
When Allan Macdiarmid died on 14 August 1945 he had been
knighted for his services and had to see his plans for Corby
come to fruition, with great expansion to follow.

47.   By 1935 most of the original plan for the works had been completed, although additions continued for a further 40 years. In the centre of the picture the three continuous weld and push bench seamless mills are complete, as are the main offices and other services.

48. View from the south showing no.1 furnace complete and work has started on no.2 furnace. The Tarmac slag in the foreground is being loaded for the crushers and wagons of crushed and sized slag for roadmaking are ready for despatch.

49. By June 1937 the fourth furnace had been completed. This was a familiar view from the back gardens of residents of Stephenson Way.

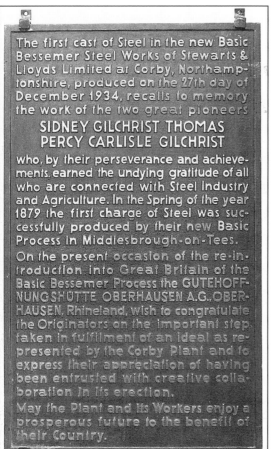

The first cast of Steel in the new Basic Bessemer Steel Works of Stewarts & Lloyds Limited at Corby, Northamptonshire, produced on the 27th day of December 1934, recalls to memory the work of the two great pioneers

SIDNEY GILCHRIST THOMAS
PERCY CARLISLE GILCHRIST

who, by their perseverance and achievements, earned the undying gratitude of all who are connected with Steel Industry and Agriculture. In the Spring of the year 1879 the first charge of Steel was successfully produced by their new Basic Process in Middlesbrough-on-Tees.

On the present occasion of the re-introduction into Great Britain of the Basic Bessemer Process the GUTEHOFFNUNGSHÜTTE OBERHAUSEN A.G., OBERHAUSEN, Rhineland, wish to congratulate the Originators on the important step taken in fulfilment of an ideal as represented by the Corby Plant and to express their appreciation of having been entrusted with creative collaboration in its erection.

May the Plant and its Workers enjoy a prosperous future to the benefit of their Country.

50.   The S&L plan for Corby was to produce mainly welded tube from Bessemer steel to counteract the German stranglehold of this product. As little expertise was available in this country to commission the Bessemer and continuous weld (Fretz-Moon) processes, a large number of German engineers were at the works for a lengthy period. It was feared that at the outbreak of the war, with so much inside information available, Corby would be a natural target. Many defensive precautions were taken including ack-ack batteries, searchlight units and smokescreens, but apart from a stray bomber or two no mass action took place. The cast-iron plaque presented in December 1934 is now on display at the East Carlton Heritage Centre.

51.   One of the five Bessemer converters being lowered with the air blast still on. The converters initially produced 20 to 25 tons of liquid steel. The blower and his team study the emitted flame which was the main means of deciding that the conversion from iron to steel was complete, following the reduction of unwanted elements. The lighter slag would be run off first and transferred to the Basic Slag Co., for processing to fertilizer. The molten metal was then poured into ladles for teeming

52.   On the teeming platform the metal was poured into ingot moulds by the teemer, in this case, Walter Hooper.

53.   View of the completed first stage of the works in 1937 with Stephenson Way in front.

54.   Seen leaving the main gate and time office, which saw the comings and goings of thousands, is the first works ambulance.

55.   Known as the 'Corby Candle' this photograph, taken at night, shows the excess coke oven gas being burnt off, with the chimneys of the plant in the background. In clear conditions the flame could be seen 12 to 15 miles away. The candle has been restored and erected in Phoenix Parkway.

56.   Vast quantities of water were required within the steelworks complex. Water was initially obtained from Thrapston gravel pits and the lakes at Blatherwycke and Deene, with the Clayholes as a reserve. The Eyebrook Reservoir was constructed and completed in 1938 and provided fishing amenities and a nature reserve. During the Second World War the reservoir was used for bombing practice by the Dambusters before their attack on the German dams.

57.   Voluntary services from first aid personnel were always encouraged by S&L. In the early years the Weldon St John Ambulance Division supplied first aiders before the S&L division was formed. An exercise is taking place at the bottom of Prestons Pit in 1936. Seen walking in the centre of the picture is David Smith.

5. The Early Town Development of the 1930s

HOUSING for the influx of thousands of men in 1933-34 was non-existent and meant that those men arriving without their families at this time found work but had to seek somewhere to sleep. A number of temporary wooden buildings were to spring up in many parts of the village which offered basic accommodation. Stories abound regarding those lucky enough to obtain lodgings where the 'hot bed' system was used, in that after an occupant left his bed in the morning it was quickly prepared for another occupant to use during the daytime; work was going on around the clock on the works site.

There are many authentic tales of men arriving at the village in those early years, having travelled by any means they could find or afford. Many came on buses along the A1 from Scotland to Stamford to reach Corby with little or no money in their pockets. Others spent several weeks walking the 300 miles even though it took several pairs of shoes. A number also cycled the distance; one who could not afford inner tubes stuffed his tyres with rags. Such was the attraction of finding work in the latter years of the Depression.

Arriving in a totally overcrowded village which, apart from four pubs, had few facilities to offer, most men quickly found that their immediate need for lodgings could not be satisfied. Finding work with S&L or a contractor was a simpler matter but involved the minimum of 12-hour day or night shifts.

During the 1933-34 winter it was thought that up to three hundred men had nowhere to sleep. The village residents were totally overwhelmed with this massive population explosion and many took in lodgers. At night time the police gave the village extra protection while men were looking for somewhere to stay. For many of the workers there was no alternative but to sleep in hedgerows, particularly in Stanion Lane where some former underground ironstone workings offered good shelter, whilst other caves were dug out of embankment faces and would often have a chimney pipe sticking out of the entrance. One cave was renowned as being lined with cardboard and covered with wallpaper; such homes, as they were, served in some cases as a base for years rather than months. One area in the village not cleared by the police at night was the parish churchyard which sometimes had up to twelve men sleeping rough.

There were no catering facilities in the village with the exception of Chapman's canteen in the wooden buildings attached to Lloyds cinema in Lloyds Road. The canteen was then moved to a site inside the main entrance to the works and offered cooked meals from 6 a.m. until the evening. The lack of washing facilities for men covered in grime was a matter which each person had to overcome.

By moving out into the surrounding villages and towns, men found lodgings at some distance but the expanding bus services alleviated this problem and, in any case, there was always the bicycle.

The Church Army was one of the first organisations to help and it built wooden huts opposite the works entrance where later was built a permanent purpose-designed block which was then extended. On the opposite side of the road, Shanks & McEwan erected wooden buildings where a large number of their employees, who had mainly come over from Ireland, were given food and a bed. Mrs. Roberts was renowned for looking after her 'boys' well but ruled them with strict discipline. S&L built permanent lodgings at the Rockingham Road/ Stephenson Way corner in their original 1934 housing scheme.

The churches of many and varied beliefs have always played a leading part in the development of the town, especially through the troubled times it had to face. From the early 1930s the existing parish and Congregational churches were involved; then the Catholic and Scottish churches were formed in 1934 and from humble beginnings were to have their permanent buildings in 1938 and 1939 respectively. Other Nonconformist churches were also involved; the Methodists built their church in the 1930s, and there has always been strong support for the Salvation Army. The Church Army will long be remembered by many men for the years of practical help with accommodation. Today over twenty churches of varied beliefs exist and work in harmony.

Whilst the Kettering Rural District Council with the County Council found the task of providing houses too much to cope with in 1933, they did provide miles of roads and services on the new estates. The K.R.D.C. explored plans for building a new town centre and investigated a district plan, but nothing came to fruition. It was suggested nationally at that time that Corby was ripe for development as a new Garden City on the lines of those already established at Letchworth and Welwyn.

It was S&L who took the lead through building societies and trust funds to provide the first 785 houses, and had to fund the next 314 because funds were not available. In 1937 a further 500 houses were started including 59 for staff at East Carlton Park. More houses were constructed and by 1939 a total of 2,253 houses had been completed. The average cost of each house including services was £400 and the rents were fixed at levels between eight and ten shillings per week, depending on the number of rooms available. It is interesting to note that in planning the sites for the new estates the company met representatives of the work force, and they preferred to be close to the works as they had been in many of the towns

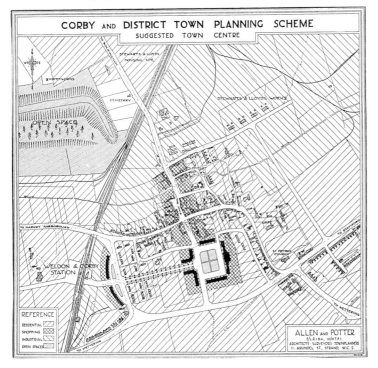

58a. The first plan for a new town centre at Corby was presented in 1934 by the architects Allen and Potter in 1934 to the Kettering District Council which projected a southern bypass and a new entrance to Corby station including commercial premises. The scheme never came to fruition as S&L built some 30 shops on their housing estates.

which they had left. This put the Stephenson Way, or Pen Green estate as it was generally known, very much in the path of prevailing winds polluted by the works.

Also provided with the Company's assistance were churches and the main shopping centre in Rockingham Road. The Recreation or Welfare Club partly opened in 1935 and was completed in 1936 by the Company with 22 acres of playing fields and the provision of the Monotech Institute for apprentice and adult education which had initially been provided at the Rowlett School.

Many alterations were also taking place in the village with new shops, the rebuilding of two of the four pubs and the provision of a site for a super cinema which was never to be built. The opening of the Odeon cinema in 1936 in Rockingham Road had made this pointless.

It was during the 1930s that Corby acquired the title of 'Little Scotland' due to the large percentage of Scottish families in the total population; many of them had the option to come to Corby when S&L closed some of their works in the Motherwell area. However, thousands of others were to come from mining areas of South Wales, West Midlands and the north, with large numbers from Ireland. In fact, many people were attracted from local villages and towns by the chance of modern housing and good pay. There was hardly a local dialect from across the nation that was not heard in Corby. Before 1933 Corby had only one Catholic family; by 1940 it had a Catholic community comprising 25 per cent of the 1939 population of some ten thousand. By 1939 it was also estimated that there were between four and five thousand Scots in the town. A tradition began then which continues to the present day: at the time of the Glasgow Fair Holiday, which took place in the second two weeks of July, there was a mass exodus of families going 'home' for the fortnight, but at the same time an influx of people from Glasgow who not only came to see their relatives, but also to view the town in which at a later date they would settle.

The original village population became a small part of the new Corby, but even now retains a certain amount of reservation about what took place in the 1930s; the industrialisation 50 years earlier had seemed sufficient for a small population's rural style of life. It is at the time of the Pole Fair that such people come into their own to show off traditions that began long before Corby became a steel town.

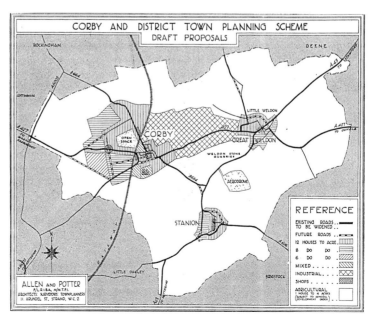

58b. The plan for the district included a number of road adjustments and an aerodrome at Cowthick, Weldon.

59a.   As the local authorities were unable to cope with the demand for houses S&L set about providing the finance from building societies and trusts. The first of 2,253 houses, mainly built by Browning Bros. of Leicester, were in Bessemer Grove where a variety of differently styled residences was constructed. Many of these were first occupied by German engineers and their families.

59b.   Before work could start on Stephenson Way estate the hedgerows of the fields had to be uprooted, 1934.

59c.   Roadways were then laid whilst work was continuing on the furnaces nearby, 1934.

59d.   The concreting crew working on what became Stephenson Way road, 1934.

60a. Building of company houses is underway off Occupation Road, running from the right of this 1936 picture, and the Welfare Club and sports ground are near completion. Occupation Farm, from which the road received its name, was demolished to make way for the water tower in Tanfields Grove. On the opposite side of the road were the makeshift huts of the Catholic church. In the top half of the picture, off the Rockingham Road, can be seen the Stephenson Way estate with the Samuel Lloyd School under construction. Half of the Rockingham Road shops are completed.

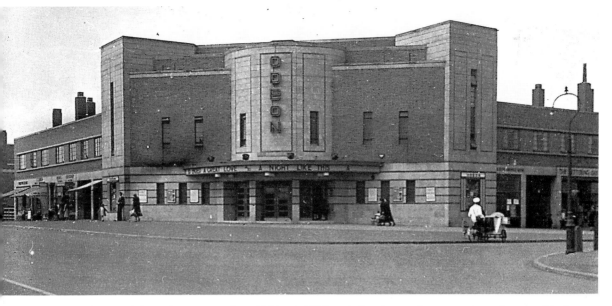

60b. The 1,042-seater Odeon cinema opened on 16 March 1936, and closed some forty years later. Seen outside the cinema is a 'Stop Me and Buy One' ice-cream salesman.

60c. The cinema's opening programme.

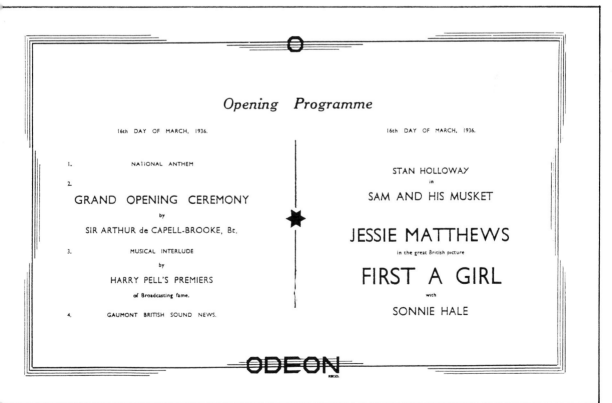

Opening Programme

16th DAY OF MARCH, 1936.

1. NATIONAL ANTHEM

2. **GRAND OPENING CEREMONY**
   by
   SIR ARTHUR de CAPELL-BROOKE, Bt.

3. MUSICAL INTERLUDE
   by
   HARRY PELL'S PREMIERS
   of Broadcasting fame.

4. GAUMONT BRITISH SOUND NEWS.

16th DAY OF MARCH, 1936.

STAN HOLLOWAY
in
SAM AND HIS MUSKET

JESSIE MATTHEWS
in the great British picture

FIRST A GIRL
with
SONNIE HALE

ODEON

61. The S&L Recreational Club, known as the Welfare, in Occupation Road, opened in 1936. The club was run by the Welfare Committee of the company. The members for 1935-36 are, *left to right, back row:* T. Rutherford, S. N. Stokes, H. Burt, W. Montgomery, A. McDougal, D. A. Russell, D. Gamble, O. Pearce, W. Marsh; *front row:* C. Butterworth, A. B. MacPhee, Com. P. F. N. Dawson R.N., W. Barr, W. Matthews, J. A. Dobie and C. B. Jamieson.

62. Officials and some members of the Urban District Council, 1945. *Left to right, back row:* George Blackhall (clerk), Mr. Marsden (sanitary), Barbara Jones (secretary), unknown, Donald Greaves (engineer); *centre row:* Rev. Brooke Westcott, Harry Underwood, Alec Easton, E. H. Gallamore, Maurice Sarrington, Alec Stewart, William Boon, Willie Young; *front row:* William Sanders, James Wallace, David Gamble, Wilfred Roe (chairman), William Rankine, Mrs. G. Payne and Bert Prentice. The members were fairly evenly split between original village people and new, mainly Scottish, arrivals. The first council offices and chamber were above the new shops in the Jamb.

63. After four years of operating from wooden buildings the Catholic church of Our Lady of Walsingham was opened on 8 November 1938. The wooden huts continued to be used for school and social purposes. The church was built on land close to where Occupation Farm stood before it was demolished.

64. The Church of Scotland, St Andrew's, was formally opened on 22 July 1939. The church had begun operating from a wooden hut in Weldon Road on 7 July 1934 and then from the church hall. The building was the last church to have been wholly built of the famed Weldon Stone which had been quarried for a thousand years. In the background of the picture can be seen the Corby Monotech Institute and the blast furnace gas holder.

65a.   The Rowlett School was grossly overcrowded in the 1930s before other schools could be completed, and a number of temporary classrooms were put on the playing field. The fact that the school was only 100 yards away from the coke ovens and gas holder presented no problems unless the wind blew from the north-east.

65b.   The Schoolhouse may ante-date the first Rowlett School, built in 1834. Some of the headmasters who lived there included Mr. Hollis and Albert Brooks who arrived in 1914. The adjoining buildings were originally the home of the Congregational church, later to become the band room for the Silver Band. Opposite was Dixon's woodyard and the popular Martin's betting office in a wooden shed.

66.	Some 24 shops were built in Rockingham Road from 1935 to 1937. The village people would say that they were going 'up to Scotland' when walking there to shop, a comment on Scottish influence in the new town. The picture in the early 1950s shows the double doors of the one time fire station. The ever popular Tipaldi's was used by both young and old, and was renowned for its cleanliness.

67.	The Samuel Lloyd School, which opened in 1937, was one of the premier buildings in the town. Repairing his cycle in this 1950 picture is the caretaker, Tom Goode, who was also senior fire officer for the town.

6. Wartime

THE OUTBREAK of the Second World War in September 1939 created many production problems for a complex that had to work 24 hours every day of the year. Many screening constructions had to be made to shield hot metal operations, to camouflage structures, and to provide air-raid shelters and an underground medical centre. From a defence angle, aerial attack was the most feared, and companies of the Royal Artillery set up searchlight units, ack-ack batteries and even barrage balloons, plus smokescreens that were operated by the Pioneer Corps. It is recorded that 25,000 gallons of paint were used to camouflage the works under the direction of the Air Ministry.

In general, a large number of employees had their jobs classified as 'reserved occupations' which meant that they were excused military service but, in addition to working long hours, they were expected to serve in one of the many voluntary organisations, such as the Home Guard, Civil Defence, Special Constabulary and so on.

Nevertheless, many young men did go off to war which led to women from the area being directed to work in the plant, not normally on the heavy side of the works as the iron and steelmaking plants were known, but in the tubeworks as crane drivers and machine operators.

Following the fall of France in 1940, the S&L chairman, Mr. Allan Macdiarmid, circulated a message to all employees which boosted morale and exhorted all to stand firm in the dark days ahead, stressing the important role of industry in providing materials for the fight. If one held firm 'victory is worth everything'.

68.　On an early afternoon in 1940 a smokescreen test was carried out on the Corby works; all departments, including every available steam loco, produced as much smoke and steam as possible. For residents of Kelvin Grove it was a lovely afternoon; not so for those in Stephenson Way. Apparently the trial was not a success; many miles of oil burners were later positioned alongside the roads around the works, the town and local villages to produce a more effective screen, which were maintained by the Pioneer Corps. Note the camouflage on gas holders and chimneys.

69a. Almost a thousand miles of three-and-a-half inch diameter seamless tubing was produced, most of it from the push bench plant at Corby under the code name 'Job 99' for the PLUTO ('Pipelines under the Ocean') operation. The lengths of tubing were taken to Tilbury where S&L built a plant to weld them into half-mile lengths. Eventually these lengths were welded together and wound on to 'conundrums', or reels, for the Royal Navy to tow across the Channel as they laid the pipe on the sea bed in the days after D-Day, 6 June 1944. Petrol was pumped through these lines which were connected to a landline system across the country from Liverpool; the landlines on the Continent were to stretch into Germany. Two lines of this type of pipe, called the HAMEL system, were laid from the Isle of Wight to Cherbourg and six lines from Dungeness to Boulogne. For the other system, called HAIS, using armoured submarine cable pipe, a total of 4,850 miles of thin steel strip was supplied by the Lancashire & Corby Steel Manufacturing Company to the Siemens company from their Corby mill. A total of 13 lines of this system were laid.

Seen in this picture inspecting the preparation of the conundrum at Tilbury in 1944 are the Prime Minister, Winston Churchill, and General Charles de Gaulle. Churchill commented later: 'Operation PLUTO is a wholly British achievement and a feat of amphibious engineering skill of which we may well be proud'.

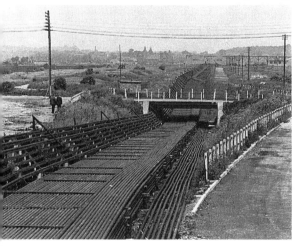

69b. One of the storage beds at Tilbury for welded lengths before being joined for winding onto the conundrum.

69c. The completed conundrum was towed out to sea by four tugs from the Royal Navy. Most of the laying operation was completed during the darkness of a single night to avoid attack from enemy aircraft. The total weight of a conundrum when loaded was 1,600 tons, as much as a battleship.

70a.   King George VI and the Queen being welcomed at Corby station by the chairman of Corby District Council and his wife, Cllr. and Mrs. Wilf Roe, on 4 March 1943. The royal party then went on a tour of the works.

70b.   The King and Queen arrive at the Research and Development laboratories in the works. Note that the car has anti-glare shields fitted to the headlamps for use during the black-out.

71a. Entertaining American airmen of the U.S.A.A.F. 401st Bombardment Group at nearby Deenethorpe airfield in 1944 were the Corby Pipe Band and the dancers of the Reg Civil and Joan Strawson School.

71b. Featured with the dancers are Betty Patrick and Danny and Charlie Murphy.

72. At Christmas 1944, the American airmen invited several hundred children from Corby and surrounding villages to a party on the base. Each airman 'adopted' a child and patiently waited in the massive queue for dinner and entertainment in the mess hall.

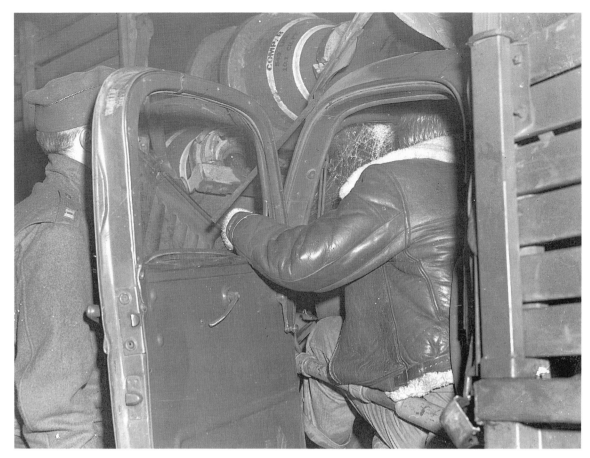

73. The narrow Church Street was the scene of many accidents, especially involving American drivers in the Second World War. Truck loads of unprimed bombs went through in regular convoys; this crash on 14 December 1944 trapped the driver in his truck.

74. The Corby police and wartime special constables are featured in this picture outside their Rockingham Road headquarters. The building was originally the offices of the Lloyds Ironstone Company which, when vacated by the police, was used as offices for the Minerals Dept. When the building was demolished in 1982, it was found to be made of Corby bricks from c.1900.

75.   Suddenly, it seemed, the war was over and, by May 1945, some 73 Flying Fortresses left the Deenethorpe airfield for operation 'Home Run' to the U.S.A. During their stay, 100 American airmen married, many choosing Corby girls as their brides. During their training in the U.S.A. and operations in the U.K., the Group lost 375 young men.

7. The Works in Post-War Years

THE PLANS for further development of the Corby site in 1939 had to be postponed until after the war, when they were re-modelled. Technical advances in sintering the ironstone and furnace control now meant that the building of new ironmaking facilities was less urgent. Much replacement and additional equipment needed to be done throughout the works. This was to include new rolling mills and tubemaking processes. The whole plan for the future meant, once again, an influx of many more employees, which led to the decision to create a New Town.

The production of the electric resistance weld (E.R.W.) tubing was to begin in 1951 with the phasing out of the push bench seamless pipe mill. In turn a new plant was built to house the plug mill which produced seamless pipe by modern methods.

These changes were only the forerunners of a vast expansion of the tubeworks to produce large tonnages of electric welded pipe incorporating a stretch process to the required sizes after the initial rolling. Large quantities of rectangular hollow sections (R.H.S.) was a further addition after earlier trials on the C.W. mills.

Methods of steel production were also to see dramatic changes in post-war years. The open hearth process began in 1949 but was superceded by a more modern process in 1971. The Bessemer steel plant closed in January 1966 once the newly-established Basic Oxygen Steel (B.O.S.) plant began operating from July 1965.

One other major change was the building of the Deene coke ovens which began in September 1961 on a new site on the works perimeter, which was eventually planned to have new ironmaking facilities.

The long-term threat of nationalisation which eventually occurred in 1967 did not put an end to all expansion but curtailed many schemes.

76.   Having joined the company in the steps of his grandfather and father, Andrew Graham Stewart eventually became chairman and general managing director of S&L in 1945 at the age of forty-four. He was to lead the company through the great expansion days of the Corby works in the 1940s and 1950s. On his death in 1965 the chairmanship reverted to the Macdiarmid family when Sir Allan's son, Neil, took until the nationalisation of the steel industry in 1967.

77.   The steelmen can be depicted in a number of ways:

a.   The model of the World's Champion Piper which showed the Scottish influence within the company. The model is made up of various sizes of pipe and fittings.

b.   As portrayed by a converter man, Sidney Hall, in the Bessemer shop showing the clothing worn to avoid metal splashes; this included at least two felt hats.

c.   The picture of Jack Greenwell, a foreman in the stripping bay and soaking pits.

d.   As portrayed in the sculpture of a steelman by the artist, Michael Grevatte, unveiled at the civic centre on 26 August 1989 by the chairman of the District Council, Cllr. Peter McGowan, and his wife.

78.   Pictured on 9 April 1952 the well-known view of the four blast furnaces from the Rockingham Road bridge. The long covering building in front of the furnaces was erected in the Second World War as a part of air-raid precautions to reduce the glow when the furnaces were being tapped.

79. A diesel-powered loco pulls a train of empty slag pots back to the blast furnaces ready for refilling. The background is the by-products section of the Glebe coke ovens. The slag was tipped down a bank at the Tarmac plant in Stanion Lane and, when cooled, was crushed for roadmaking materials.

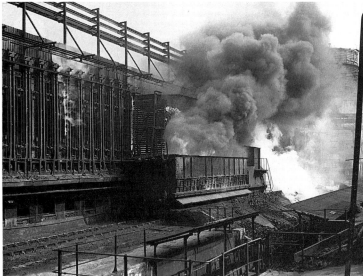

80. The red hot coke is being pushed from the Glebe coke ovens where it was produced from coal. The coke falls into a transfer car from which it is loaded for use in the blast furnaces. Apart from valuable gas produced by this process, many chemical by-products were also recovered. A total of over 26 million tons of coke was made at the works site from 1934 to 1980.

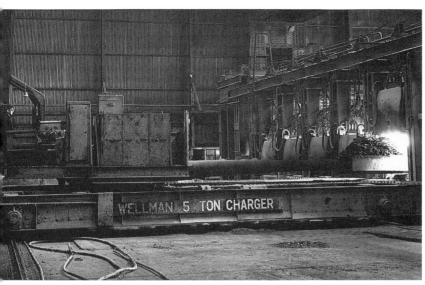

81. The two open hearth furnaces which produced high quality steel used hot molten iron and scrap steel as raw materials. The plant closed on 7 September 1971, having been open since 8 December 1949.

82. The open hearth produced around one hundred tons of molten steel which would be teemed from a ladle through a central trumpet that fed into the bottom of the ingot moulds.

83. The electric arc furnaces came into operation in 1939 and 1940 and were later able to produce 40-ton casts of specialised steel. The plant was the last of the steelmaking plants to close when it ceased production on 21 December 1980.

84.   The heavy mill was the first of a number of mills that would roll the reheated ingots into bars for further processing. The mill was later replaced by a more modern one.

85.   The red hot bars have been through the tandem and continuous mills. The next stage is to roll the bars into a strip prior to tubemaking.

86.   The last stands of the no.1 strip mill seen in 1969 with the roller, Robert Mackie, on the left and the assistant roller, Theo Workman, in the centre. Many major alterations were to take place on this mill in later years.

87.   The narrow strip mill shows strip awaiting coiling ready for the next process, making small sizes of welded tubes.

88.   Aerial view of the works in 1959, viewed from the village.

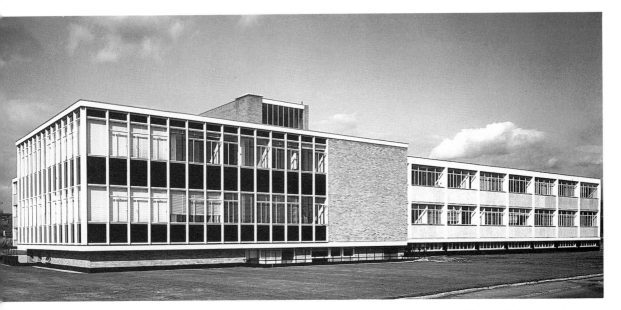

89. An integral part of the S&L division, with tubemaking plants around the country as well as at Corby, was the research and technical development centre. The new building of the D.R. & T.D. opened at the main entrance to the works in 1958. It was later extended and later renamed the Technical Centre; it closed in March 1991.

90. The no.4 continuous weld mill came into operation in September 1948. The steel strip, which came through six furnaces in a continuous length, was then formed into a tube by a series of rolls which completed the weld at high temperature. A flying saw seen in the picture cut the pipe to length; its speed was between 120 and 720 feet per minute. The four mills could produce over half a million tons a year. From 1960 the mills began to produce rectangular hollow sections in addition to circular tubing.

91. Another train load leaves the continuous weld warehouse in 1950. Remains of the barbed wire entanglements, which surrounded the works perimeter in the Second World War, can be seen in the background.

92. Work begins on the plug mill seamless pipe site in June 1952. The remainder of the infilled site towards Weldon was later covered by other tubemaking mills. The plug mill closed down in 1992.

93.   Over the years of iron and steel activity some thousands of apprentices attended the Training Centre, the Monotech Institute and the Technical College to complete their courses. The great experience they gained in the works, combined with expert tuition, led to qualified engineers being in demand in many parts of the world. Seen seated outside his beloved centre in 1951 is Dr. Ernie Taylor, area training officer, with his assistant Jim Watson on his right and Tom Prattis to his left.

94a. The long service certificate awarded by S&L showed the Scottish influence within the company. The beautifully coloured decoration is headed by the Glasgow coat of arms and the other arms illustrate the company's links with other parts of the world.

94b. This group of Minerals Department certificate recipients in 1965 are: Bill Hudson (40 years), Ivan Fellows (43 years), John Sharman (50 years) and Bert Fellows (50 years).

95. By 1971 issue of the long service certificate had ceased. Gold watches were presented to this group at Brigstock Manor, the headquarters of the Minerals Department, by the manager, Norman Kitchen, seated on the right of the lady recipient.

96. Perhaps the last aerial view of the complete works site, taken on 17 May 1974. The site was almost two miles long and over a mile wide. The only main feature to be added later were the sinter plant extensions and chimneys. In the bottom right corner is the newly completed dual carriage Tunwell loop, and work is taking place on the A427 Corby to Weldon road to make it dual carriageway.

8. New Town Development

IMMEDIATELY THE WAR ended even more housing was needed and Corby Urban District Council undertook the task by expanding the Lloyds estates to the west and north; by 1952 prefabricated bungalows were included among the 1,500 properties which were to serve their purpose for 40 years. The estates also included several neighbourhood shopping centres. Great care was taken at that time, and in the years since, to preserve the remnants of the Rockingham Forest within the town boundary which give a pleasing entrance to the town from the south and west.

The further expansion plans within the works meant that the population was set to rise to 40,000, and the government made Corby a New Town in 1950 along with others in the country. The Corby Development Corporation was formed to bring this about. The corporation carried out its initial planning from headquarters set up in Fineshade Abbey, some six miles away towards Stamford. As the new town centre was constructed, the corporation was sited in the main street which became known as Corporation Street.

At this time up to 1,000 people travelled daily from Kettering to work in Corby with about five hundred women travelling to Kettering for work. Surveys on the Rockingham Road bridge showed that over five hundred cyclists passed at each peak hour.

The next 30 years changed all the travelling patterns, with new roads and new estates. Few cyclists were visible as the motor car filled the road system. The town became the 'taxi town' of England with, at one time, more taxis per head than any other town.

The corporation expanded the town to the south-west, which stretched from the town centre for a distance of over two miles; 2,800 homes were built, an increasing number of which were private.

The duties of the Development Corporation were considered complete in 1979 with the population then at 50,000, and the Commission for the New Towns took over to build vast industrial estates and factories. The housing stock of the corporation was transferred to the (then) district council, which sold several thousands of their total stock to tenants.

97.   The new Rockingham Road bridge opened as shown looking towards the village. The traffic and pedestrian flow indicates that the photograph was taken at a shift change in the works. The Corringdon lorry was one of a large fleet of a locally based company.

98. The Corringdon transport company was formed by the merger of a number of local companies with its headquarters at the Hunters Manor, Weldon. The company name incorporated elements of the names of Corby, Kettering and Weldon, where it had depots as well as at Ketton and Thrapston. The company's long distance section was nationalised in 1949 but it later recovered some of this activity. In August 1971 the company closed down. The photograph of its fleet and drivers and owners was taken in the winter of 1948 on the Kettering Town Football Club car park.

99. The scene at Clayholes Field in 1950. Amongst the children are Tony and David Sykes, Mary Martin, Phyllis Bates and Beryl Robinson. Not long after the photograph was taken the area was developed as the St James' Industrial Estate.

100.	A scene of concentration in the Mission and Reading Room in Church Street in the 1950s. *From left to right:* Mr. George Wardle, Mr. Ted Bloomfield, Mr. Albert Wright and Mr. Edward 'Jummy' Lattimore.

101.   After the parish church, this is perhaps the oldest building in the town. Standing in the High Street it was originally built in 1609, and was restored and re-thatched by the Development Corporation.

102.   Taken in the early 1950s, this picture shows the most hallowed piece of turf in the town. The Welfare Club bowling green was much appreciated by players and spectators.

103. Church Street in the 1950s shows the *Black Horse* pub. Within a year or two, the whole street was demolished.

104. A scene from the back garden of a house in the bottom of Stephenson Way in the early 1950s, as the electric shovel clears the overburden in Earlstrees Quarry.

105.   The curved sweep of the Studfall Avenue shops which opened in 1950. Opposite the shops at one time was the first open air market which existed before the town centre was built in the early 1950s.

106.   This view, taken in May 1961, shows the Jamb having undergone many changes; only the shops and house on the left remain from the original view. The first council offices were above the shops on the right; the new *Cardigan Arms* can be seen further from the left and still belonged then to Smiths of Oundle.

107.   There were few traffic problems in 1961 in the new and expanding town centre. Corporation Street was part of the new centre built by the Development Corporation. The police station can be seen at the end of the street.

108.   In June 1964 the Priors Hall golf course, which had been created by S&L and the Urban District Council on restored quarry land, was prepared in readiness for public use. After 25 years the course is as popular as ever and is landscaped with hundreds of well-established trees.

109a.   The once derelict rectory was restored as the Hightrees Scout Centre and opened by Lt. Col. John Chandos-Pole, Lord Lieutenant for the county, on 23 November 1969.

109b.   Seen introducing the Lord Lieutenant to Roy Burton is Dr. Tony Hall Turner, the Commissioner for the Rockingham District Scouts. In the background is Cllr. Kelvin Glendenning, chairman of the Urban District Council.

110.   Originally built as the Air Raid Precautions (A.R.P.) headquarters, these buildings became Corby's first public library in 1948. Later they were used as a museum. The building was at the junction of Rockingham Road and Pen Green.

111.   Not long after its opening in November 1960 the library was amalgamated with the county technical library. Half the building was destroyed by fire on 24 March 1979 along with a vast number of books and records.

112.   The Farmstead Road neighbourhood shopping centre was opened in 1960. As can be seen, many of the flats had yet to be let.

113. Pictured from the *Strathclyde Hotel, c.*1970, is the town centre, looking north-east to the works in the background. The Church of the Epiphany is in the centre of the picture.

114.   By May 1969 the land of Earlstrees Quarry had been restored and building had commenced. In the foreground to the left are the trial houses of White Post Court with the factories of British Sealed Beams and Golden Wonder shown above them. On the right is part of the estates built by the Urban District Council, including the prefabricated bungalows erected in Maple Grove after the Second World War.

115.   The photograph of the town in 1974 demonstrates how it has expanded. The major road leading out of town to the top of the picture is Westcott Way, named after a former rector who served on the Urban District Council. Part of the road follows the original Roman road from Leicester.

116. Before the opening of the Festival Hall, the Welfare Club offered the largest premises for functions. For Christmas and New Year the hall was decorated for the seasonal events; these included the Staff Dance, the pensioners' Christmas treats and the annual Grand Draw.

117. The S&L Pipe Band was formed in the 1930s and became very famous in a county in which it was a total novelty. It is seen here leading the Carnival parade, c.1975. For 25 years a Highland Gathering has been held in the town and in 1972 the town staged the World Pipe Band Championship.

118a.   The Corby Town Football Club, whose team was known as the 'Steelmen', was founded in 1948. Its entry into the Midland League in the 1952-53 season was most memorable, as it came second to Nottingham Forest Reserves. In October 1952 the team met Kettering Town at home in the second qualifying round of the .A. Cup, and a crowd of 9,800 paid a record £491 to see a draw, the Steelmen eventually winning the replay at Kettering. In the next round a gate of 10,239 saw the team draw at home to Peterborough United with receipts of £799. The Steelmen lost the replay.

The team that season was, from left, *back row:* George Poole, Alf Horne, Horace Hinton, Tommy Hadden, Jimmy Garvie, Jack Connors; *front:* Alex Laird, Danny Smith, Colin Senior, Barry Matthews, Fred Slater.

118b.   The S&L Rugby Club was formed in 1936. This followed what was thought to be the first ever game of rugby to be played at Corby when a representative team from the county played a Buckinghamshire county team on the West Glebe playing field. One of the most successful club teams was that of 1951/2 which went 43 matches without defeat. *From left to right, back row:* Ken Gould, Johnny McRoberts, Ian Baird, Andy Bald, Jim Moody, Jack Adamson, Alan Southwell, Bill Lorrimer, John Drane, Tommy Classick; *front row:* Martin Moon, Bob Morrison, Arthur Savage, Bill Davies, Tommy Frayne.

9. Quarrying in the Post-War Years

QUARRYING in the Corby area, which had begun in 1880 by uncovering the ironstone bed and removing it manually, was to take, quite literally, giant steps once the war was over. Mechanical means of removing overburden and ironstone began before the turn of the century with the introduction of many novel pieces of machinery which proved sufficient for working 30-ft. quarry depths. A series of Ransomes and Rapier electric face shovels was purchased in the 1930s and these reliable work-horses proved their worth by tackling quarries 60-ft. deep and more with the assistance of other machines.

With plentiful reserves of ironstone buried at even greater depths in the surrounding countryside, a series of giant walking draglines was used after the Second World War. These were capable of operating to depths in excess of one hundred feet. The first machine purchased was a Bucyrus Eyrie from America which began operating in 1950, and the first British machine built by Ransomes and Rapier began operating in 1951 at Priors Hall quarry. Two further machines were built locally by the same company, one at Cowthick quarry, Weldon in 1960, and one at Great Oakley quarry in 1963. Finally, in 1974 a redundant machine was walked from Rutland to work at Harringworth quarry.

Some of the statistics connected with these machines give an idea of their immensity: total weight—1,650 to 1,800 tons; boom or jib length—280 to 300 ft.; height of boom top from ground—190 ft.; bucket capacity—over thirty tons; with each step of the feet the machine moved seven feet.

An initial order had been placed with Ransomes and Rapier in the 1970s for an even greater machine than these monsters but, because of the continuing rationalisation within the steel industry at that time, it was never undertaken.

Whilst these walking draglines took the limelight, many other crews and machines were employed in the quarry system such as the borers which drilled for samples and blasting, the rock diggers who loaded the ironstone into wagons and the steam and diesel locomotives whose crews, at one time, pulled their trains over 45 miles of railway tracks in the Minerals Department area.

119a.   The Earlstrees scene of April 1958 shows the Ransomes and Rapier electric face shovel removing the overburden and, in the foreground, the Ruston Bucyrus rock shovel waiting to load a train of wagons with ironstone. In the background are the houses of Stephenson Way and the silhouette of the blast furnaces.

19b. Operating at Brookfield Quarry are the face shovel and the stone digger. Note the area of the ironstone bed which has been drilled in a pattern and charged with explosive to loosen the ironstone.

119c. The old gave way to the more modern in Rockingham Pit on 12 March 1948 as the steam-powered shovel retires in favour of the rebuilt electric face shovel.

120.   This 1964 view shows a
shallow outcrop ironstone bed
at Shotley Quarry close by
Harringworth. In the
background is the opposite side
of the Welland Valley.

121.   The first British large
walking dragline, the Ransomes
and Rapier W1400, was built
off the Gretton Road from
Weldon between 1949 and
1951. An American Bucyrus
Erie walking dragline was
already operating nearby in
1950. The W1400 is seen
making a cutting alongside the
A43 Weldon to Stamford road.
On the right can be seen the
Weldon sewerage works and, at
the top centre, Bottom Lodge
Farm, one of many to disappear
in the search for ironstone.

122. The deep Priors Hall Quarry is a complete picture of quarrying activity. Below the dragline is a machine boring into the quarry face to loosen the rock by blasting. In the foreground another machine is loading ironstone, which had been drilled and blasted to loosen it, into wagons to take to the works.

123a. Parts for the huge walking draglines which operated in the Corby area were obtained from many sources. Seen in early 1959 leaving the works of Sir William Arrol & Co., Glasgow is a component at the start of its long journey to the Cowthick Quarry at Weldon.

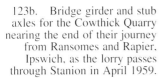

123b. Bridge girder and stub axles for the Cowthick Quarry nearing the end of their journey from Ransomes and Rapier, Ipswich, as the lorry passes through Stanion in April 1959.

123c. The 'A' frame member coming up Haunt Hill at Weldon on 15 May 1959, within a mile of Cowthick Quarry, after its journey from Glasgow.

124. Special arrangements were made on 25 September 1971 to close the A43 trunk road from Northampton to Stamford when the W1400 walked backwards (as usual) from Cowthick quarry to begin work in Barns Close quarry . Within two to three hours of this 1,700-ton giant crossing, the road was re-opened completely undamaged.

125. The last of the walking draglines to be built was the W1800 at Great Oakley, seen ready to take its first steps in 1963. The machine had a weight of 1,767 tons and a boom length of 282 ft. comprised of S&L pipe.

126a. To move a walking dragline, named Sundew, from the redundant quarry at Exton Park, Rutland, to Harringworth near Corby, involved a journey of 13 miles. The walk began on 30 May 1974 and was completed just over two months later on 8 August having crossed many obstacles including rivers, roads and railways. The event attracted media attention and thousands of spectators. A special report was filmed by B.B.C. television for the *Blue Peter* programme, with John Noakes at the controls. After six years' work at the quarry the machine was again made redundant and eventually cut up for scrap.

126b. Some of the crew involved in the move are pictured here: Cecil Mason, Tansley Huffer (the driver), Maurice Brown (project manager), Ron Hill (project foreman) and Fred Abbot.

127.   Whilst vast tonnages of limestone used in the smelting processes came from Derbyshire, thousands of tons were
excavated from Longhills quarry, Weldon. For some forty years the quarrying was done manually using the 'plank and
barrow' method of extraction. In later years a crushing plant was set up on the site, which today is the venue for the
Sunday open air market.

128. The scene in the market square on 19 June 1961 when the town officials were introduced to Her Majesty, Queen Elizabeth II. In the background, building is about to begin on the Church of the Epiphany.

129. Following the visit to the town, the royal party arrived at the works where the Queen and Duke of Edinburgh were greeted by Mr. Andrew Stewart, chairman and general managing director of S&L, and the director of the Corby site, Mr. W. C. Bell.

S BSC TUBES
CORBY WORKS GROUP
Open Week
JUNE 30 – JULY 7

1977

THE QUEEN'S SILVER JUBILEE

NORTHAMPTONSHIRE COUNTY COUNCIL

QUEEN ELIZABETH SCHOOL
CORBY

Occasion of the
NAMING CEREMONY
by
HER MAJESTY THE QUEEN

12 November 1982

---

130. To mark the Silver Jubilee of the Queen, complex arrangements were made for conducted tours of the works. Many hundreds of families took advantage of this invitation to visit the heavy and hot working sections of the massive industrial complex.

131. As part of the royal visit to the county, Queen Elizabeth II paid a visit to Corby to name the Queen Elizabeth School in Oakley Road.

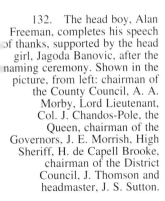

132. The head boy, Alan Freeman, completes his speech of thanks, supported by the head girl, Jagoda Banovic, after the naming ceremony. Shown in the picture, from left: chairman of the County Council, A. A. Morby, Lord Lieutenant, Col. J. Chandos-Pole, the Queen, chairman of the Governors, J. E. Morrish, High Sheriff, H. de Capell Brooke, chairman of the District Council, J. Thomson and headmaster, J. S. Sutton.

11. *Nationalisation and the Aftermath*

FOR A NUMBER of years the iron and steel industry nationwide faced possible nationalisation and this eventually took place on 28 July 1967.

As was to be expected, its full implementation took some time and many companies held on to their name as long as possible. With a vast industry to control, the British Steel Corporation, which employed about a quarter of a million people, found that both costs and competition rose and soon a period of rationalisation began. One of its early victims was the Lancs. & Corby cold strip mill at Corby which employed 450 people. A much heralded White Paper on the 10-year strategy for the Corporation was presented by the Secretary of State for Trade and Industry, John Davies, in February 1973 and Corby was amongst the plants indicated as having a limited future. Paragraph 59 read:

> Corby has a long term future as a major tube making plant, and steelmaking will continue there at least for the rest of the present decade. The steelworks is the major employer in the town and a final decision on the future of steelmaking will be taken in the course of the next few years in consultation with those concerned.

133.   The Minister of Power, Richard Marsh (second from right), seen on a visit to Corby when the nationalisation of the steel industry was completed after the first attempt by the Labour government in 1949 had failed. This photograph was taken in 1967 outside the main entrance of S&L with some members of the Board of Directors. Left to right: Peter Matthews, Richard Otley and, finally, Neil Macdiarmid who was then chairman and general managing director of the company. The prediction of the chairman, who had led the company in a vigorous campaign against nationalisation, that the company would, like the phoenix, rise again from the ashes, was never realised.

134a.   A period of rationalisation followed the nationalisation of the industry, which led to the first works closure, by the Strip Division, of the Lancs. & Corby in September 1971. This is the main bay of plant which employed 450 people. Identified as operating the two cold reversing rolling mills are: Fred Dix on the left at the control desk, Len Aplin facing the mill, Jimmy Murray looking towards the camera from the desk of the other mill, and Paul Lee at the other desk.

134b.   This new Schloemann cold reversing mill was installed at the Lancs. & Corby in 1964. From left to right the operators pictured are: Peter Bergen, Len Aplin, Willie McCullum and Arthur Portman.

12. Closure and Clearance

THE DECISION was reached in 1979 that iron and steelmaking operations at Corby were to be closed and the news came as an unbelievable shock to the town which was almost totally dependent on the industry.

The pros and cons of the decision are still being debated but, in the event, the plant began to shut down during the three-month national steel strike which started on 2 January 1980. The 1973 Government White Paper on the steel industry indicated that, because of a large world and European over-capacity, harsh decisions were to come. The Steel Corporation decided to plan a small number of production sites near the coast where imported ore of a high iron content could reduce costs dramatically.

Certainly in the latter years the costs at Corby had risen for a number of reasons, including the high cost of ironstone extraction from ever greater depths, escalating fuel costs for conversion into iron, and rising labour costs. Since the closure of the iron and steelmaking operations, for the Corby tubeworks the cheaper supply of raw materials from the north-east coast has guaranteed a long-term future.

Perhaps one of the most impressive sights in the 1980s was the way the huge industrial site was cleared and soon a vast array of new units brought to an end the 50-year history of a complex which at one time was the largest of its kind in Europe. That it had 100 miles of railway track within the site was an indication of its immensity.

The total production statistics in tonnages for the iron and steel complex at Corby from 1934 to 1980:

Ore crushing	94,503,266
Coke ovens	26,234,000
Blast furnace iron	30,879,525
Bessemer steel	17,944,908
Open hearth steel	4,394,625
Basic oxygen (B.O.S.) steel	11,149,239
Electric furnace steel	2,324,652
Heavy rolling mills	32,535,736

135.   The initial announcement that iron and steelmaking at Corby was to cease was made on 9 February 1979. An action group, R.O.S.A.C. (Retention of Steelmaking at Corby) was formed and on 19 September it organised a massive protest march from the works to the town centre, involving some 10,000 people, on the day that British Steel was to meet the trade unions at Corby. After years of speculation the closure was confirmed on 1 November 1979. Part of the protest march is seen along the Weldon Road on its way to the town centre.

136.   A notice at the entrance to the amenity block of the Basic Oxygen steelmaking plant expressed the sadness felt by all across the huge complex at that moment when men were to disperse and, in many cases, would never see one another again.

137.   To advise thousands of people across the whole site who were to lose their jobs, a team of representatives, headed by Harry Eastwood, was trained as counsellors. Seen with the team outside the special village of Portacabins is Alan Hanley, senior closure counsellor; on his left on the bottom step is another counsellor, Frank Thorpe.

138.   By May 1980 the iron and steelmaking complex was almost completely closed. For nearly 50 years this had been a scene of smoke, steam, machine activity and, above all, manpower, and had never been seen so clear or so quiet.

139.   Demolition began with the midday explosions on Sunday, 2 August 1980, which sounded the death knell of one of the first structures: the coke oven gas holder.

40a.   Over 48 years since it was first lit, the no.1 blast furnace had a decided tilt after partial demolition.

140b.   The no.1 blast furnace was detonated on Guy Fawkes' day, 5 November 1981.

140c.   Most of the site clearance was undertaken by Thos. W. Ward Ltd. of Sheffield.

141.   The former open hearth and B.O.S. process buildings, which between them had produced 15 million tons of steel, are shown being demolished in November 1981.

13. Rising from the Ashes

THE RECOVERY of the town in the 1980s, from high unemployment and low morale, began with the mutual co-operation of all elements of authority in the town, county and nationally. Much of its redevelopment can be traced to the Joint Industrial Development Committee set up during those early days, comprising people closely associated with the problem and led from the beginning by Corby District Council. As the town had been granted Assisted Area status in 1979, grants of over £130 million were made from the European Community and more from government and other sources.

When the Enterprise Zone scheme was begun nationally, the town had its initial application turned down, but an appeal to the then Environment Minister, Michael Heseltine, revoked the Government's initial rejection, and by June 1981 the minister opened the first of several such zones. In the past few years the town has been cited as an example to many others, both in this country and worldwide, who have had to face up to the loss of their sole industry.

Plans are now being formulated to bring Corby into the 21st century; a town that is no longer dependent on one industry, but on a broad-based economy, with a vastly improved environment to that of a steel town.

The 20th century began with a small rural village adjusting to a newly-introduced industry of ironstone quarrying and brickmaking for its population of about a thousand people. It will go into the 21st century as a town of about sixty thousand which has come through a traumatic century. Who knows what lies in store for the next hundred years?

142.   By 1988 the site clearance was almost complete, and this view shows a dramatic change from that of the previous 50 years. One of the first of many commercial outlets and industrial units to be built was the Asda store which opened on 10 November 1986 and is seen in the centre of the photograph. At the top, in the distance, is Kirby Hall.

143.   R.S. Components have proved to be one of the most successful companies to move into one of the Enterprise Zones set up with government help following the 1980 closure of iron and steel activities. Situated on the Weldon (North) Industrial Estate, the company is the second largest industrial employer in the town with some 1,800 people on its staff. The large extension to the complex, shown here, was completed in 1992.

144.   One of the earliest factories to be built on the Earlstree Estate after the works closure was the flour mills.

145. An earlier view of the Eurosugar plant on the Weldon (North) Estate.

146. By September 1984 a vast amount of industrial development had occurred. In the restored Earlstree estate, pictured, over two million square feet of buildings had been erected. The background shows the opposite side of the Welland Valley with the village of Caldecott and the Eyebrook Reservoir.

147. To mark the association of Corby and its twinned town in France, the sheltered accommodation off the Rowlett Road, built in 1987, is named Chatelleraut Court. Corby is also twinned with Velbert in Germany.

148. The original open space in the town centre was used as the market place and, over the years, for many outdoor events.

149.   In 1991 the market place saw a dramatic change; the market moved into Queens Square to make way for shops and offices which were opened in 1992.

150.   Moving into the 21st century, the long-term project is to build a gas-fired power station which will generate electrical power sufficient for a medium-sized city. The plant is being built on land reclaimed from quarrying, as are most of the industrial estates.

Select Bibliography

Corby has been fortunate that in the past years a number of historians have researched and published their own findings. In particular my access to the following reading sources is gratefully acknowledged:

Alexander, A. W., *The Foundations of a Steel Town* (Corby Historical Society, July 1969)

Alexander, A. W. and York, M. R., *The Handloom Weavers of Corby* (Corby Historical Society, November 1968)

Allen, E. G., *Town and Country Planning*, Vol. II, no. 7 (May 1934)

British Steel Corporation: Ten Year Development Strategy (H.M.S.O., February 1973)

Corby Development Corporation, *Corby New Town—Master Plan* (December 1952)

Corby Development Corporation, *Programme for the Visit of Queen Elizabeth II* (1961)

Corby District Council, *Corby Works* (1989)

Elliott, Colin, *The Generalities of Corby*

Mawdsley, W., *Corby's Elizabethan Charter 1585* (1981)

Pettit, P. A. J., *The Royal Forests of Northamptonshire* (1968)

Scopes, Sir Frederick, *The Development of Corby Works* (1968)

Sharman, Michael, *Some Notes on the History of Corby* (1980)

Stokes, Dr. Arthur, *Souvenir of Corby Pole Fair* (1922)

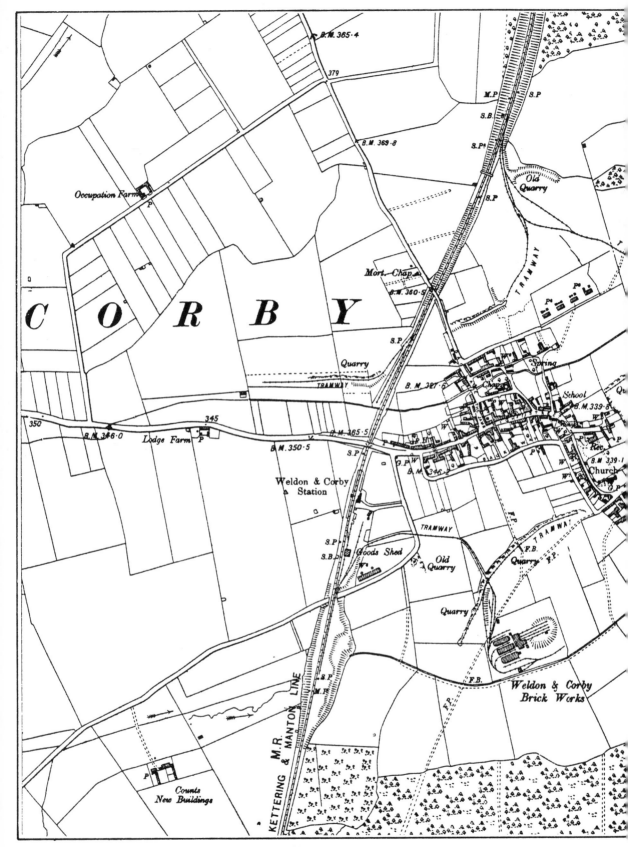

Detail from Ordnance Survey map of the Corby area, 1901.